D1709499

ACADIA
National Park

BY CHRISTINA LEAF

BELLWETHER MEDIA • MINNEAPOLIS, MN

Blastoff! Discovery launches a new mission: reading to learn. Filled with facts and features, each book offers you an exciting new world to explore!

BLASTOFF! UNIVERSE

BLASTOFF! Beginners
GRADE K

BLASTOFF! READERS
GRADES 1-3

BLASTOFF! DISCOVERY
GRADE 4

This edition first published in 2023 by Bellwether Media, Inc.

No part of this publication may be reproduced in whole or in part without written permission of the publisher.
For information regarding permission, write to Bellwether Media, Inc., Attention: Permissions Department,
6012 Blue Circle Drive, Minnetonka, MN 55343.

Library of Congress Cataloging-in-Publication Data

Names: Leaf, Christina, author.
Title: Acadia National Park / by Christina Leaf.
Description: Minneapolis, MN : Bellwether Media, Inc., 2023. |
  Series: Blastoff! Discovery : U.S. national parks | Includes bibliographical
  references and index. | Audience: Ages 7-13 | Audience: Grades 4-6 |
  Summary: "Engaging images accompany information about Acadia National
  Park. The combination of high-interest subject matter and narrative text
  is intended for students in grades 3 through 8"– Provided by publisher.
Identifiers: LCCN 2022016469 (print) | LCCN 2022016470 (ebook) |
  ISBN 9781644877517 (library binding) | ISBN 9781648347979 (ebook)
Subjects: LCSH: Acadia National Park (Me.)–Juvenile literature.
Classification: LCC F27.M9 L53 2023 (print) | LCC F27.M9 (ebook) |
  DDC 974.1/45–dc23/eng/20220414
LC record available at https://lccn.loc.gov/2022016469
LC ebook record available at https://lccn.loc.gov/2022016470

Editor: Betsy Rathburn
Series Design: Jeffrey Kollock   Book Designer: Laura Sowers

Printed in the United States of America, North Mankato, MN.

TABLE OF CONTENTS

SUNRISE ON CADILLAC MOUNTAIN

It is a clear night in Acadia National Park. Two hikers
click on their headlamps as they walk up a thickly forested trail.
Though it is August, the pine-scented air is chilly. The hikers
pause at the edge of the forest to look up. Thousands of stars
speckle the sky.

FIRST IN THE NATION

Between October and March, Cadillac Mountain is the first place you can see the sunrise in the United States.

After a few hours, the hikers reach the top of Cadillac Mountain, Acadia's highest peak. Small groups of people are milling around. Soon, a rosy glow peeks over the water below. The sun bathes everything in pinks and yellows as it rises into the sky. Welcome to Acadia National Park!

ACADIA NATIONAL PARK

Acadia National Park is the easternmost national park in the **continental** United States. It was the first national park created east of the Mississippi River. This small park covers around 77 square miles (199 square kilometers) in eastern Maine, near the small town of Bar Harbor.

Acadia is a coastal park. Most of Acadia lies on Mount Desert Island in the Atlantic Ocean. A smaller part of the park is on the Schoodic **Peninsula**. This section of **mainland** lies to the east, across the Mount Desert Narrows. Part of Isle au Haut and other, smaller islands also fall within the park's boundaries.

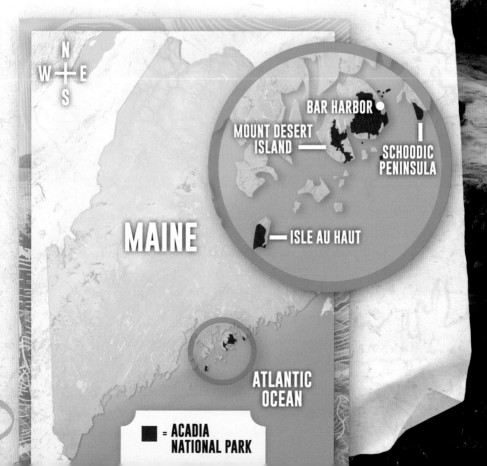

N
W + E
S

BAR HARBOR ●

MOUNT DESERT
ISLAND —

SCHOODIC
PENINSULA

— ISLE AU HAUT

MAINE

ATLANTIC
OCEAN

■ = ACADIA
NATIONAL PARK

MOUNT DESERT ISLAND

BAR HARBOR

7

THE LAND

GRANITE

AN ISLAND PARK

Heavy glaciers once covered Acadia. The land sank under them, and ocean water rushed in. This turned Acadia's mountains into islands. Later, the land rose again as the glaciers moved on. But lakes and rivers remain.

Acadia began to form more than 500 million years ago. Mud and **volcanic** ash were squeezed together to form **metamorphic** rock. Later, layers of sand, silt, and ash created **sedimentary** rocks such as sandstone and siltstone. **Magma** cooled to create **igneous** rocks such as the granite of Cadillac Mountain and pink granite along the coast.

Glaciers also helped shape Acadia. These massive sheets of ice carved valleys and wore down mountains. They helped create Acadia's rivers and lakes.

The park's landscape is still changing. Waves and wind wear away its rocky shores. Ice freezing and thawing widens the cracks in Acadia's granite.

HOW ICE BREAKS DOWN GRANITE

1. Water flows into cracks in granite.

3. The ice melts and the granite breaks apart.

2. The water freezes and expands, making cracks bigger.

Mountains cover much of Acadia. On the eastern side of Mount Desert Island, the tallest mountaintops are bare rock. Forests cover Acadia's valleys and the low mountains on the western side. The park is on the border between **deciduous** and **boreal** forest zones. Many of the forests are a mix of both. Wetlands are scattered throughout the park. Rocky cliffs line Acadia's coast.

NO DESERTS HERE

Explorer Samuel de Champlain named Mount Desert Island. It came from the French *Île de Monts Déserts*, or "Island of Barren Mountains."

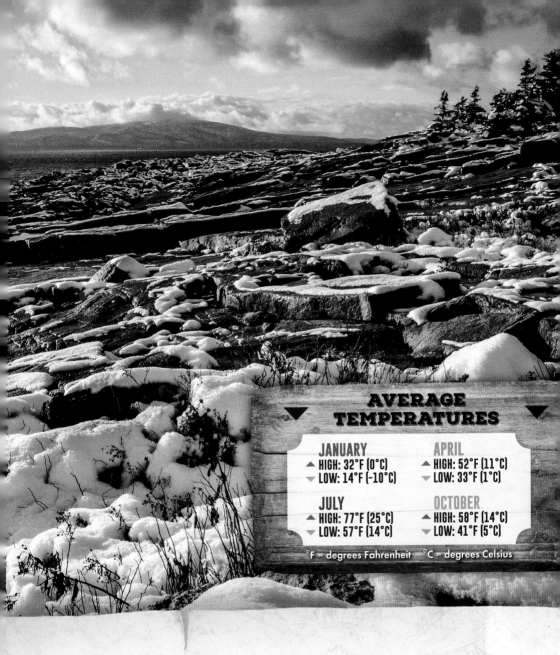

AVERAGE TEMPERATURES

JANUARY
▲ HIGH: 32°F (0°C)
▼ LOW: 14°F (-10°C)

APRIL
▲ HIGH: 52°F (11°C)
▼ LOW: 33°F (1°C)

JULY
▲ HIGH: 77°F (25°C)
▼ LOW: 57°F (14°C)

OCTOBER
▲ HIGH: 58°F (14°C)
▼ LOW: 41°F (5°C)

°F = degrees Fahrenheit   °C = degrees Celsius

Acadia has four seasons. Chilly falls are followed by snowy winters that often have temperatures below freezing. **Nor'easters** may dump a lot of snow. Springs are usually cool and foggy. Acadia's warm summers are cooled by ocean breezes.

PLANTS AND WILDLIFE

Acadia's many landscapes are home to a wide variety of plants and animals. Ferns blanket forest floors. Foxes and bobcats hunt for snowshoe hares between fir and spruce trees. White-tailed deer dash through birches and maples. At night, bats and barred owls take to the skies.

Acadia's freshwaters are home to many animals, too. Beavers build dams while loons call from the water. Minks hunt for trout in the streams. Frogs croak among the cattails in wetlands, and painted turtles sun themselves along lakeshores. Damselflies rest on water lilies and lobelia that bloom in Acadia's lakes.

RED FOX

BARRED OWL

AMERICAN MINK

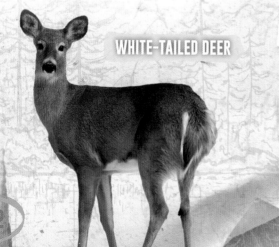

WHITE-TAILED DEER

DAMSELFLY

MOOSE-ING IN ACTION

Maine has large populations of both moose and black bears. But few visitors to Acadia spot these large mammals. No moose and few black bears make homes on Mount Desert Island.

SNOWSHOE HARE

Life Span: up to 5 years
Status: least concern

snowshoe hare range = ⬛

LEAST CONCERN	NEAR THREATENED	VULNERABLE	ENDANGERED	CRITICALLY ENDANGERED	EXTINCT IN THE WILD	EXTINCT
▲						

Acadia is famous for its ocean wildlife. Harbor and gray seals sun themselves on the park's rocky shores. Porpoises and humpback whales swim farther out. Seabirds such as terns and puffins search for fish, while sandpipers wade in shallow waters. Lobsters and clams hide below the surf.

GRAY SEAL

SEA STAR

ATLANTIC PUFFIN

Life Span: more than 20 years
Status: vulnerable

Atlantic puffin range = ▮

LEAST CONCERN	NEAR THREATENED	VULNERABLE	ENDANGERED	CRITICALLY ENDANGERED	EXTINCT IN THE WILD	EXTINCT

▲

   Low tide exposes a rich world of wildlife in Acadia's **tide pools**. Many kinds of seaweed and **algae** blanket the rough rocks. Sea stars hunt for mussels in the pools. Anemones and sea urchins cling tightly to the rocks. Cast-off shells of periwinkle snails give hermit crabs new homes.

HUMANS IN ACADIA NATIONAL PARK

People have lived in and around Acadia for more than 12,000 years. Around 9,000 years ago, it became home to the Wabanaki people. This group of tribes is made up of the Maliseet, Micmac, Penobscot, and Passamaquoddy.

PEOPLE OF THE DAWN LAND

Wabanaki means "people of the dawn land." Their name is inspired by the sunrise on Cadillac Mountain.

CADILLAC MOUNTAIN SUNRISE

MICMAC WIGWAM

The Wabanaki moved between inland forests and the coast. They hunted deer in Acadia's forests and collected clams and other shellfish from the coast. They used birch bark to build **wigwams** and sturdy canoes. The Wabanaki people lived in small groups. They used Mount Desert Island as a place to meet up and trade with one another.

In 1604, Samuel de Champlain and Pierre Dugua, Sieur de Monts of France, explored what is now Acadia National Park. Soon, other French explorers made their way to the area. The Wabanaki were slowly forced out of the area by wars, diseases, and new settlers.

In the 1800s, visitors called "rusticators" came to enjoy the beauty of the area. By 1901, the land was getting bought up by wealthy families such as the Rockefellers. George B. Dorr worried this would limit who could visit. He worked to buy up land in order to preserve the area.

GEORGE B. DORR

PRESIDENT
WOODROW WILSON

Many of the landowners gave land to the cause. In 1916,
President Woodrow Wilson set aside the land as Sieur de Monts
National Monument. It became Lafayette National Park in 1919,
and was finally renamed Acadia in 1929.

Today, Acadia is one of the most visited national parks in the country. In recent years, around 4 million people have visited annually. Wabanaki people continue to visit the area. Some sell handmade baskets and other crafts. The Abbe Museum just outside the park teaches visitors about Wabanaki history and **culture**.

ABBE MUSEUM

SAND BEACH

VISITING ACADIA NATIONAL PARK

There is something for everyone at Acadia National Park! Miles of trails lead hikers through forests, up mountains, and along the coast. Bicyclists pedal on Acadia's historic carriage roads. Bird-watchers search for the more than 300 species found in the park. Brave visitors scale Acadia's cliffs. In winter, skiers glide across the snow.

KAYAKING

TEA AND CARRIAGES

You do not have to be outdoorsy to enjoy Acadia! Visitors can take a horse-drawn carriage ride to see the park. Many people enjoy afternoon tea and popovers at Jordan Pond House.

TOP SITES

JORDAN POND HOUSE

BASS HARBOR
HEAD LIGHT STATION

THUNDER HOLE

SAND BEACH

Acadia offers plenty of opportunities to appreciate the ocean! Visitors watch waves crash at Thunder Hole. Families search for wildlife in tide pools. Swimmers brave the chilly water at Sand Beach. Kayakers paddle around Acadia's rocky coves. Boats take hopeful visitors out on whale-watching tours.

PROTECTING THE PARK

Acadia is one of the most crowded national parks. This affects the park in many ways. Cars pollute the air and can harm plants and wildlife. People pollute by leaving trash. Even hiking can harm **ecosystems** if people step on plants or bother animals. Other pollutants come from nearby factories. These leave harmful chemicals in Acadia's waters.

Climate change also impacts Acadia. Rising temperatures on land and in the water can ruin homes for plants and animals. Warmer temperatures will make snow less common. Sea levels rising from climate change will cause landmarks like Thunder Hole and Sand Beach to disappear.

DARK NIGHTS

Acadia is one of the few places on the East Coast with little light pollution. Reducing light helps animals that are most active at night. Groups are working with communities to keep Acadia's nights dark.

People can help protect Acadia. Visitors can stick to the "leave no trace" program by picking up all trash before leaving an area. Staying on the trails prevents harm to plants and wildlife. Taking the park shuttle can reduce pollution from cars.

LEAVE NO TRACE

People can also help to reduce climate change. Electricity often comes from harmful fuels. Turning off lights and electronics when they are not needed can use less of these fuels. Walking or riding a bike instead of taking a car can also help. If we work together, we can keep Acadia beautiful for many years to come!

SHUTTLE

RIDING BIKES

ACADIA NATIONAL PARK FACTS

Area: **77** square miles
(199 square kilometers)

Area Rank: **50**TH
largest park

Date Designated:
February 26, 1919
(as Lafayette National Park)

January 19, 1929
(renamed Acadia National Park)

Annual Visitors:
4 million in 2021

Population Rank: **6**TH
most visited park in 2021

Highest point:
Cadillac Mountain;
1,530 feet (466 meters)

TIMELINE

AROUND 7000 BCE

The Wabanaki
live in the area

1916

President Woodrow Wilson
creates Sieur de Monts
National Monument

1604

Frenchmen Samuel de Champlain
and Pierre Dugua, Sieur de Monts,
explore the area

FOOD WEB

BOBCAT

SNOWSHOE HARE

AMERICAN MINK

TROUT

PLANTS

DAMSELFLY LARVAE

1928

The Abbe Museum
is built

1919

The area becomes
Lafayette National Park,
and is renamed Acadia
in 1929

1947

A major wildfire burns
more than 16 square miles
(41 square kilometers)
of Acadia

GLOSSARY

algae—plants and plantlike living things; most kinds of algae grow in water.

boreal—related to northern forests that grow in cold regions; boreal forests are often filled with pines, firs, and other coniferous trees.

climate change—a human-caused change in Earth's weather due to warming temperatures

continental—related to part of a continent; the continental United States includes all states except Hawaii.

culture—the beliefs, arts, and ways of life in a place or society

deciduous—related to trees that lose their leaves each year

ecosystems—communities of living things that include plants, animals, and the environments around them

glaciers—massive sheets of ice that cover large areas of land

igneous—related to a type of rock that forms when melted rock inside the earth called magma cools

magma—melted rock within the earth

mainland—the main part of a country or continent

metamorphic—related to a type of rock that forms from heat and pressure

nor'easters—large storms that hit coastal northeastern states; winds blow in from the northeast.

peninsula—a section of land that extends out from a larger piece of land and is almost completely surrounded by water

sedimentary—related to a type of rock that forms from layers of sediment that are pressed together; sediments are tiny pieces of rocks, minerals, and other natural materials.

tide pools—pools of ocean water left when the tide goes out

volcanic—related to a volcano; a volcano is a hole in the earth that erupts hot ash, gas, or melted rock called lava.

wigwams—cone-shaped homes made with bark or animal skins covering a structure of wooden poles

TO LEARN MORE

AT THE LIBRARY

Grack, Rachel. *Maine*. Minneapolis, Minn.: Bellwether Media, 2022.

Ogintz, Eileen. *The Kid's Guide to Acadia National Park*. Camden, Maine: Down East Books, 2019.

Payne, Stefanie. *National Parks: Discover All 62 Parks of the United States*. New York, N.Y.: DK Publishing, 2020.

ON THE WEB

FACTSURFER

Factsurfer.com gives you a safe, fun way to find more information.

1. Go to www.factsurfer.com.

2. Enter "Acadia National Park" into the search box and click 🔍.

3. Select your book cover to see a list of related content.

INDEX